21st Century
Basic Skills
Library

KIDS CAN MAKE MANNERS COUNT
PLAY FAIR!

3

by Katie Marsico

Cherry Lake Publishing • Ann Arbor, Michigan

Published in the United States of America
by Cherry Lake Publishing
Ann Arbor, Michigan
www.cherrylakepublishing.com

Content Adviser: Tonia Bock, PhD, Associate Professor of Psychology,
St. Thomas University, St. Paul, Minnesota

Photo Credits: Cover and pages 1, 4, 6, 8, 14, 16, 18, and 20,
©Denise Mondloch; page 10, ©photobank.ch/Shutterstock, Inc.;
page 12, ©iStockphoto.com/buzbuzzer

Library of Congress Cataloging-in-Publication Data
Marsico, Katie, 1980–
  Play fair! / by Katie Marsico.
    p. cm. — (21st century basic skills library) (Kids can make manners
count)
  Includes bibliographical references and index.
  ISBN 978-1-61080-438-7 (lib. bdg.) —
ISBN 978-1-61080-525-4 (e-book) — ISBN 978-1-61080-612-1 (pbk.)
1. Fairness—Juvenile literature. 2. Play—Juvenile literature.
3. Etiquette for children and teenagers—Juvenile literature. I. Title.
  BJ1533.F2M37 2013
  395.1'22—dc23   2012001712

Cherry Lake Publishing would like to acknowledge
the work of The Partnership for 21st Century Skills.
Please visit www.21stcenturyskills.org for more information.

Printed in the United States of America
Corporate Graphics Inc.
July 2012
CLFA11

TABLE OF CONTENTS

Cheating at Checkers

Every Friday Jack played checkers with his friend Beth.

He was older and knew the game's **rules** better.

Jack loved winning!

Sometimes Beth thought Jack did not play fairly.

She caught him **cheating** by moving pieces when he was not supposed to.

This made Beth sad and angry.

Making Manners Work

Jack liked playing checkers with Beth.

He hated to lose, though.

Mrs. Jones was their teacher. She offered Jack and Beth a few **suggestions**.

Mrs. Jones said that playing fairly was important.

Playing fairly was a way to **practice** good **manners**.

She reminded Jack that cheating hurts people's feelings.

Jack played fairly at other times.

He followed the rules when he played football.

He also followed the rules when he played card games.

Being a Better Player

Jack needed to play fairly in all the games he played.

A person did not really win if he cheated. That's what Mrs. Jones told Jack.

Jack understood the game better than Beth did. Mrs. Jones said that was no reason to trick Beth.

Mrs. Jones discussed the rules of checkers again.

Jack sometimes offered to help Beth.

He answered her questions truthfully.

They talked about what they had learned after each game.

Soon Beth became better at checkers.

Jack played more fairly. He still enjoyed the game as much as ever.

Good manners made them both winners!

Find Out More

BOOK

Graves, Sue, and Desideria Guicciardini (illustrator). *Not Fair, Won't Share*. Minneapolis: Free Spirit Publishing, 2011.

WEB SITE

KidsHealth—Cheating
kidshealth.org/kid/feeling/school/cheating.html
Learn more about the importance of playing fair and what happens if a person cheats.

Glossary

cheating (CHEE-ting) purposely breaking or changing the rules to win

manners (MA-nurz) behavior that is kind and polite

practice (PRAK-tis) to do something regularly

rules (ROOLZ) guidelines that players in a game must follow

suggestions (sug-JES-chunz) advice or ideas

Home and School Connection

Use this list of words from the book to help your child become a better reader. Word games and writing activities can help beginning readers reinforce literacy skills.

a	cheating	he	moving	really	this
about	checkers	help	Mrs.	reminded	though
after	did	her	much	rules	thought
again	discussed	him	needed	sad	times
all	each	his	no	said	to
also	enjoyed	hurts	not	she	told
and	ever	if	of	sometimes	trick
angry	every	important	offered	soon	truthfully
answered	fairly	in	older	still	understood
as	feelings	Jack	other	suggestions	was
at	few	Jones	people's	supposed	way
became	followed	knew	person	talked	what
being	football	learned	pieces	teacher	when
Beth	Friday	liked	play	than	win
better	friend	lose	played	that	winners
both	game	loved	player	that's	winning
by	games	made	playing	the	with
card	good	making	practice	their	work
caught	had	manners	questions	them	
cheated	hated	more	reason	they	

Index

About the Author

Katie Marsico is an author of children's and young-adult reference books. She lives outside of Chicago, Illinois, with her husband and children.